EXIT THE KING

A Play

by

EUGENE IONESCO

Translated by

DONALD WATSON

SAMUEL FRENCH

LONDON

NEW YORK   TORONTO   SYDNEY   HOLLYWOOD

EXIT THE KING

Presented by the English Stage Company at The Royal Court
Theatre, London, on the 12th September 1963, with the following
cast of characters:

(in the order of their appearance)

THE GUARD	*Peter Bayliss*
KING BERENGER THE FIRST	*Alec Guinness*
QUEEN MARGUERITE	*Googie Withers*
JULIETTE	*Eileen Atkins*
QUEEN MARIE	*Natasha Parry*
THE DOCTOR	*Graham Crowden*

Directed by GEORGE DEVINE

Designed by JOCELYN HERBERT

*The action of the Play passes on a morning in the dilapidated throne-room
of King Berenger the First's crumbling palace*

EXIT THE KING

SCENE—*The dilapidated throne-room of King Berenger the First's crumbling palace. Morning.*

The walls show the remaining signs of past glory, but are now in a state of ruin and cracked, a particularly large crack appearing in the wall R. The back wall is curved and has small arched entrances up R and up L. There are double, swing doors down R and a single swing door down L, all in poor condition. There is a window L. There are star traps in the floor R and L. The walls down R and down L are set forward of the back run, leaving wide, masked exits R and L for use when the thrones RC and LC are struck; for the entrance and exit of the wheel-chair, and to provide easy exits if the traps are not practical. A large throne, with two or three steps leading up to it, is on a revolving rostrum up C. Two smaller thrones, on tracks, are RC and LC. There is a clock in the wall over the door down L. Radiators for central heating are against the wall below the doors down R and down L.

When the CURTAIN *rises, the* GUARD *is standing at the foot of the throne up* C. *He carries a halberd and has three plaques for fixing to the backs of the thrones. He attaches the first plaque, being King Berenger's cipher, to the throne up* C *then stands* R *of the throne.*

GUARD (*announcing*) His Majesty the King Berenger the First. Long live the King! (*He salutes*)

(KING BERENGER THE FIRST *enters down* R. *He wears a deep crimson cloak and a crown. He carries a sceptre. He crosses rapidly and exits up* L)

(*He goes to the throne* RC *and puts on a label, then announces*) Her Majesty Queen Marguerite, First Wife to the King, followed by Juliette, Domestic Help and Registered Nurse to their Majesties. Long live the Queen! (*He salutes*)

(QUEEN MARGUERITE *enters down* L.
JULIETTE *follows her on.* MARGUERITE *has a crown on her head and is wearing a royal purple cloak that is rather old.*
MARGUERITE *and* JULIETTE *exit down* R)

(*He goes to the throne* LC *and puts on a label, then announces*) Her Majesty Queen Marie, Second Wife to the King, but first in affection, followed by Juliette, Domestic Help and Registered Nurse to their Majesties. Long live the Queen! (*He salutes*)

(QUEEN MARIE *enters down* R.
JULIETTE *follows her on.* MARIE *appears younger and more beautiful than Marguerite. She has a crown and a royal purple cloak. She is wearing jewels. Her cloak is of more modern style and looks as if it comes from a high-class couturier.*

MARIE *crosses and exits down* L.
JULIETTE *exits up* R.
The DOCTOR *enters up* R)

His Notability, Doctor to the King, Gentleman Court Surgeon, Bacteriologist, Executioner and Astrologist.

(*The* DOCTOR *crosses to* C, *and then, as though he had forgotten something, turns and exits up* R)

(*He remains silent for a few moments. He looks tired. He moves down* R, *rests his halberd against the wall and blows into his hands to warm them*) I don't know, this is just the time when it ought to be hot. Central heating, start up! (*He pauses*) Nothing doing. Central heating, start up! (*He feels the radiator down* R) Radiator's stone cold. It's not my fault. He never told me he'd taken away my job as Chief Firelighter. Not officially, anyway. You never know with them. (*He suddenly picks up his halberd, and salutes*)

(MARGUERITE *enters up* R *and crosses to* C. *She looks rather severe.*
JULIETTE *follows her on, carrying a milk bucket, a broom and a duster. She puts the bucket and broom against the wall* R)

GUARD. Long live the Queen!
MARGUERITE (*to Juliette; looking around*) There's a lot of dust about. And cigarette ends on the floor.
JULIETTE (*picking up some cigarette ends from the floor*) I've just come from milking the cow, Your Majesty. She's almost out of milk. I haven't had time to do the sitting-room. (*She goes to the throne* RC *and dusts it*)
MARGUERITE. This is *not* the sitting-room. It's the throne-room. How often do I have to tell you?
JULIETTE. All right, the throne-room, as Your Majesty wishes. I haven't had time to do the sitting-room.
MARGUERITE (*to the Guard*) It's cold.
GUARD. I've been trying to turn the heat on, Your Majesty. (*He moves to* R *of Marguerite*) Can't get the system to function. The radiators won't co-operate. The sky is overcast and the clouds don't seem to want to break up. The sun's late.

(JULIETTE *dusts the throne up* C)

And yet I heard the King order him to come out.
MARGUERITE. Is that so!

(JULIETTE *dusts the throne* LC)

The sun's already deaf to his commands.
GUARD. I heard a little rumble during the night.

(JULIETTE *moves down* L *and dusts the radiator*)

There's a crack in the wall.
MARGUERITE. Already? Things are moving fast. I wasn't expecting this so soon.

GUARD. Juliette and I tried to patch it up.
JULIETTE. He woke me up in the middle of the night.
GUARD. And now it's there again. Shall we have another try?
MARGUERITE. It's not worth it.

(*The* GUARD *returns to his place down* R)

We can't turn the clock back. (*To Juliette*) Where's Queen Marie?
JULIETTE (*moving* LC) She must still be dressing.
MARGUERITE. Naturally!
JULIETTE. She was awake before dawn.
MARGUERITE. Oh! Well, that's something.
JULIETTE. I heard her crying in her room.
MARGUERITE. Laugh or cry, that's all she can do. Let her be sent for at once. (*To Juliette*) Go and fetch her.

(JULIETTE *crosses towards the door down* R)

GUARD. Long live the Queen! (*He salutes*)

(MARIE *enters up* L *and moves* R *of the throne* LC *to* C. MARGUERITE *and* JULIETTE *curtsy*)

MARGUERITE (*moving to* R *of Marie*) Your eyes are quite red, my dear. It spoils your beauty.
MARIE (*tearfully*) I know.
MARGUERITE. Don't start crying again.
MARIE. I can't really help it.
MARGUERITE. Don't go to pieces, whatever you do. What's the use? It's the normal course of events, isn't it? You were expecting it. Or had you stopped expecting it?
MARIE. You've been waiting for it. (*She weeps*)
MARGUERITE. Fortunately. Like that, everything's in order. (*To Juliette*) Oh, give her another handkerchief.

(JULIETTE *crosses to* L *of Marie, takes her soiled handkerchief, gives her a clean one, then moves down* L)

MARIE. I was still hoping . . .
MARGUERITE. You're wasting your time. (*She shrugs*) Nothing but hope on their lips and tears in their eyes. What a way to behave!
MARIE. Have you seen the doctor again? What did *he* say?
MARGUERITE. What you've heard already.
MARIE. Perhaps he's made a mistake.
MARGUERITE. Don't start hoping all over again. There's no mistaking the signs——
MARIE. Perhaps he's misinterpreted them.
MARGUERITE. —if you look at them objectively. And you know it.

(*The* GUARD *points at the crack in the wall* R)

MARIE (*looking at the wall*) Oh, that crack!

MARGUERITE. Oh, you've seen it, have you? And that's not the only thing. It's *your* fault if he's not prepared. It's *your* fault if it takes him by surprise. *You* let him go his own way. You've even led him astray. (*She crosses above Marie to* L *of her*) Oh, yes. Life was very sweet. With your fun and games, your dances, your processions, your official dinners, your winning ways and your firework displays, your silver spoons and your honeymoons. How many honeymoons have you had?

MARIE (*turning to her*) They were to celebrate our wedding anniversaries.

MARGUERITE. You celebrated them four times a year. "We've got to *live*," you used to say. But one must never forget.

MARIE. He's so fond of parties.

MARGUERITE. People know, and carry on as if they didn't. They know and they forget. But *he* is the King. *He* must not forget. *He* should have his eyes fixed in front of him, know every stage of the journey, know exactly how long the road, and never lose sight of his destination.

MARIE (*moving* RC) My poor darling, my poor little king. (*She weeps*)

MARGUERITE (*to Juliette*) Give her another handkerchief.

(JULIETTE *crosses to Marie, takes her soiled handkerchief, gives her a clean one, then returns down* L)

(*To Marie*) Be a little more cheerful, can't you? Tears are catching. He's weak enough already. (*She moves to* L *of Marie*) What a pernicious influence you've had on him. But there! I'm afraid he liked you better than me, but I wasn't at all jealous. I just realized he wasn't being very wise. And now you can't help him any more. (*She crosses above Marie to* R *of her*) Look at you. Bathed in tears. You've lost that challenging look. Where's it all gone, that brazen insolence, that sarcastic smile? (*She crosses above Marie to* L *of her*) Come on, now, wake up. Take your proper place and try to straighten up. Think! You're still wearing your beautiful necklace. Come along, take your place.

MARIE. I'll never be able to tell him.

MARGUERITE. *I'll* see to that. (*She moves to the throne* RC) I'm used to the chores.

MARIE (*moving to the throne* LC) And don't *you* tell him, either. Please. Don't say a word, I beg you.

MARGUERITE. Please leave it to me. (*She sits on the throne* RC) We'll still need you, you know, at various moments of the ceremony. You like ceremonies.

MARIE. Not this one. (*She sits on the throne* LC)

MARGUERITE (*to Juliette*) You—spread our trains out properly.

JULIETTE. Yes, Your Majesty. (*She crosses to Marguerite and spreads her train*)

MARGUERITE. I agree it's not so amusing as your charity balls. Those dances you get up for the young folks, and old folks, and newly-weds. For victims of disaster or the honours list. For lady novelists. Or charity balls for the organizers of charity balls. This one's just for the family, with no dancers and no dance.

MARIE. Don't tell him. It's better if he doesn't notice anything.

MARGUERITE. And goes out like a light? That's impossible.

(JULIETTE *crosses to Marie and spreads her train*)

MARIE. You've no heart.

MARGUERITE. Oh, yes, I have. It's beating.

MARIE. You're inhuman. He's not prepared.

MARGUERITE. It's your fault if he isn't. He's been like one of those travellers who linger at every inn, forgetting each time that the inn is not the end of the journey. When I reminded you that in life we must never forget our ultimate fate, you told me I was a pompous blue-stocking.

JULIETTE (*aside*) It *is* pompous, too. (*She stares at Marguerite*)

MARGUERITE (*to Juliette*) What's the matter with *you*, goggling at us like that? You're not going to break down, too, I hope. You can leave us.

(JULIETTE *moves to the door down* L)

Don't go too far away, we'll call you.

JULIETTE. So I don't have to do the sitting-room now?

MARGUERITE. It's too late. Never mind. Leave us.

(JULIETTE *exits down* L)

MARIE (*rising and moving* C) Tell him gently, I implore you. Take your time. He might have a heart attack.

MARGUERITE. We haven't the time to take our time. This is the end of your happy days, your high jinks, your bean-feasts and your strip-tease. You've let things slide to the very last minute and now we've not a minute to lose. Obviously. It's the last. We've a few moments to do what ought to have been done over a period of years. You've still got a part to play, don't worry. I'll tell you when to leave us alone. After that, I'll help him.

MARIE (*moving down* LC) It's going to be so hard. So hard.

MARGUERITE. As hard for me as for you, and for him. Stop grizzling, I say. That's a piece of advice. That's an order.

MARIE. He won't go!

MARGUERITE. Not at first.

MARIE. I'll hold him back.

MARGUERITE (*rising*) Don't you dare! (*She moves to* R *of Marie*) It's got to pass off decently. Let it be a success, a triumph. It's a long time since he had one. (*She crosses down* L) His palace is crumbling. His fields lie fallow. His mountains are sinking. (*She moves to* L *of Marie*) The sea has broken the dykes and flooded the country. He's let it all go to rack and ruin. You've driven every thought from his mind with your perfumed embrace. How I hated that perfume.

Such bad taste. But that was him all over. Instead of consolidating the land, he's let acre upon acre plunge into the bowels of the earth.

MARIE. Expert advice on how to stop an earthquake.

MARGUERITE. I've no patience with you. He could still have consolidated—planted conifers in the sand and cemented the threatened areas. But, no! Now the kingdom's as full of holes as a gigantic Gruyére cheese.

MARIE. We couldn't fight against fate, against natural phenomena like erosion.

MARGUERITE (*crossing to the Guard*) Not to mention all those disastrous wars.

(*The* GUARD *looks at Marie*)

While his drunken soldiers were sleeping it off, at night, or after a a lavish lunch in barracks——

(*The* GUARD *snaps to attention*)

—our neighbours were pushing back our frontiers, our national boundaries shrinking. His soldiers didn't want to fight.

MARIE. They were conscientious objectors.

MARGUERITE. He called them conscientious objectors here at home. The conquering armies called them cowards and deserters, and they were shot. (*She moves down* RC) You can see the result: towns razed to the ground, burnt-out swimming pools, abandoned *bistros*. The young are leaving in hordes. At the start of his reign there were nine thousand million inhabitants.

MARIE. Too many. There wasn't room for them all.

MARGUERITE. And now there are only about a thousand old people left. Less. Even now, while I'm talking, they're passing away.

MARIE. There are forty-five *young* people, too.

MARGUERITE (*moving to* R *of Marie*) No-one wants *them*. *We* didn't want them either; we were forced to take them back. Anyway, they're ageing rapidly. Repatriated at twenty-five, two days later and they're over eighty. You can't pretend that's the normal way to grow old.

MARIE. But the King, *he's* still young.

MARGUERITE. He *was* yesterday, he *was* last night. (*She moves to the throne* RC *and sits*) You'll see in a moment.

GUARD (*announcing*) His Notability, the Doctor, has returned. His Notability, His Notability!

(*The* DOCTOR *enters down* R. *The door opens and closes by itself. He looks like an astrologer and executioner at one and the same time. On his head he is wearing a pointed hat with stars. He is dressed in red with a hood hanging from the collar. He has a magnifying glass on a cord round his neck and carries a large telescope*)

DOCTOR (*crossing to* C *and bowing to Marguerite*) Good morning, Your Majesty. (*He bows to Marie*) Good morning, Your Majesty. I hope your Majesties will forgive me for being rather late. I've come straight from the hospital, where I had to perform several surgical operations of the greatest import to science.

MARIE (*moving to* L *of the Doctor*) You can't operate on the King.

MARGUERITE. You can't *now*, that's true.

(*The* DOCTOR *looks at Marguerite, then at Marie*)

DOCTOR. I know. Not his Majesty.

MARIE. Doctor, is there anything new? He *is* a little better, isn't he?

(*The* DOCTOR *crosses down* L)

Isn't he? He *could* show *some* improvement, couldn't he?

DOCTOR. He's in a typically critical condition that admits no change.

MARIE. It's true, there's no hope. (*She looks at Marguerite*) *She* doesn't *want* me to hope, she won't *allow* it.

MARGUERITE. Many people have delusions of grandeur, but you're deluded by triviality. There's never been a queen like you. You make me ashamed for you.

(MARIE *turns away* L)

Oh! She's going to cry again.

DOCTOR (*crossing to* R *of Marie*) In point of fact, there *is*, if you like, *something* new to report.

MARIE. What's that?

DOCTOR (*moving* C) Something that merely confirms the previous symptoms. Mars and Saturn have collided.

MARGUERITE. As we expected.

DOCTOR. Both planets have exploded.

MARGUERITE. That's logical.

DOCTOR. The sun has lost between fifty and seventy-five per cent of its strength.

MARGUERITE. Naturally.

DOCTOR. Snow is falling on the North Pole of the sun. The Milky Way seems to be curdling. The comet is exhausted, feeling its age; winding its tail round itself and curling up like a dying dog.

MARIE. It's not true, you're exaggerating. You must be. Yes, you *are* exaggerating.

DOCTOR. Do you wish to look through the telescope?

MARGUERITE. There's no point. We believe you.

(MARIE *moves to the throne* LC *and sits*)

What else?

DOCTOR. Yesterday evening it was spring. It left us two hours and thirty minutes ago. Now it's November. Outside our frontiers, the grass is shooting up. The trees are turning green. The cows are calving twice a day. Once in the morning and again in the afternoon about five, or a quarter past. (*He crosses down* L) Yet in our country, the brittle leaves are peeling off. The trees are sighing and dying, and the earth is quaking rather more than usual.

GUARD (*announcing*) The Royal Meteorological Institute calls attention to the bad weather conditions.

MARIE. I can feel the earth quaking. I can hear it.

MARGUERITE. It's that crack, getting wider, spreading.

DOCTOR. The lightning's stuck in the sky, the clouds are raining frogs, the thunder's mumbling. That's why we can't hear it. Twenty-five of our countrymen have been liquified. Twelve have lost their heads. Decapitated. This time, without my surgical intervention.

MARGUERITE. Those are the signs, all right.

DOCTOR. Moreover . . .

MARGUERITE (*interrupting*) No need to go on. It's what always happens in a case like this. We know.

GUARD (*announcing*) His Majesty, the King!

(*Royal music is heard.* MARGUERITE *and* MARIE *rise. The* DOCTOR *moves to* R *of Marguerite*)

Attention for His Majesty. Long live the King! (*He salutes*)

(*The* KING *enters up* L. *He has bare feet.*

JULIETTE *follows the King on. The* KING *crosses to the foot of the throne* C. JULIETTE *crosses and stands down* R *of the throne* RC. *She is carrying the King's slippers*)

MARGUERITE. Now where has he scattered his slippers?

JULIETTE. Sire, they are here.

MARGUERITE. It's a bad habit to walk about barefoot.

MARIE (*to Juliette*) Put his slippers on. Hurry up! He'll catch cold.

(JULIETTE *crosses to the King and puts his slippers on*)

MARGUERITE. It's no longer of any importance whether he catches cold. It's just that it's a bad habit.

DOCTOR (*with a humble and courteous bow*) May I be allowed to wish Your Majesty a good day. And my very best wishes.

MARGUERITE. That's nothing now but a hollow formality.

(JULIETTE *crosses to* R)

KING (*turning to Marie*) Good morning, Marie. (*He turns to Marguerite*) Good morning, Marguerite. Still here? I mean, you're here already. How do you feel? *I* feel awful. I don't know quite what's wrong with me. My legs are a bit stiff. I had a job to get up, and my feet hurt. I must get some new slippers. Perhaps I've been growing. (*He sits on the throne* C) I had a bad night, what with the earth splitting, frontiers retreating, cattle bellowing and sirens screaming. There's far too much noise. I must look into it. We'll see what we can do.

(MARGUERITE *and* MARIE *sit on their thrones*)

(*He winces*) Ouch, my ribs. (*He turns to the Doctor*) Good morning, Doctor. Is it lumbago?

(MARGUERITE *and the* DOCTOR *look at each other*)

I'm expecting an engineer—from abroad. Ours are no good nowadays. They just don't care. Besides, we haven't any. Why did we close the Polytechnic?

(*The* DOCTOR *is about to reply*)

Oh, yes. It fell through a hole in the ground. And why build another when they all disappear? I've got a headache. (*He looks towards the window*) Clouds. I thought I'd banished clouds. Clouds! We've had enough rain. Enough, I said! Enough rain. There's an idiotic cloud, like an old man, weak in the bladder. (*To Juliette*) What are you staring at me for? You're very red in the face today. My bedroom's full of cobwebs. Go and get rid of them.

JULIETTE. I've done it once today. I don't know where they spring from. They keep on coming back.

DOCTOR (*to Marguerite*) You see, Your Majesty. This, too, confirms my diagnosis.

KING (*rising and crossing to* L *of Marie*) What's wrong with you, my love?

MARIE (*stammering*) I don't know—nothing—nothing wrong.

KING. You've got rings round your eyes. Have you been crying? Why?

MARIE. Oh, God!

KING (*to Marguerite*) I won't have anyone upset her. And why did she say "Oh, God!" like that?

MARGUERITE. It's an expression. (*To Juliette*) Go and get rid of those cobwebs.

KING (*moving down* L) Those cobwebs, disgusting!

MARGUERITE (*to Juliette*) Hurry up, don't dawdle! Have you forgotten how to use a broom?

JULIETTE (*collecting her bucket and broom*) Mine's worn out. I need a new one. I could really do with twelve brooms.

(JULIETTE *crosses and exits up* L. *There is a pause.* MARIE, *the* DOCTOR *and* MARGUERITE *stare at the King*)

KING. What are you all staring at me for? Is there something abnormal about me? It's so normal to be abnormal—there's no such thing as abnormality. (*He crosses to* C, *limping a little*) So that's straightened out.

(MARIE *rises and rushes to* L *of the King*)

MARIE. My dear King, you're limping.

(*The* KING *takes a pace or two* RC *and back, limping a little*)

KING. Limping? *I'm* not limping. I *am* limping a little.
MARIE. Your leg hurts. I'm going to help you along.
KING. It doesn't hurt. Why should it hurt? (*He moves up* C) Why, yes, it *does*, just a little. It's nothing.

(MARIE *moves to* L *of the King*)

(*To Marie*) I don't need anyone to help me. Though I like being helped by you.
MARGUERITE (*rising*) Sire, I have some news for you.
MARIE. No, be quiet!
MARGUERITE. Keep quiet yourself.
MARIE (*to the King*) What she says isn't true.
KING. News about what? *What* isn't true? Marie, why do you look so sad? What's the matter with you?
MARGUERITE. Sire, we have to inform you that you are going to die.
DOCTOR (*moving a step down* RC) Alas, yes, Your Majesty.
KING. But I know that, of course I do. We *all* know it. You can remind me when the time comes. Marguerite, what is this? You have a mania for disagreeable conversation early in the morning.
MARGUERITE. It's midday already.
KING. It's not midday. (*He looks at the clock*) Why, yes, it is. No matter. I haven't eaten anything, yet. Let my breakfast be brought. To tell the truth, I'm not very hungry. (*He moves to* L *of the Doctor*) Doctor, you'll have to give me some pills to stimulate my appetite and shake up my liver. My tongue's all coated, isn't it? (*He shows his tongue to the Doctor*)
DOCTOR. Yes, indeed, Your Majesty.
KING. My liver's choked up. I had nothing to drink last night, but I've a nasty taste in my mouth.
DOCTOR. Your Majesty, Queen Marguerite has spoken the truth. You *are* going to die.
KING. You get on my nerves. I'll die, yes, I'll die all right. (*He moves down* LC) In forty, fifty, three hundred years. Or even later. When I want to, when I've got the time, when it suits me. Meanwhile, let's get on with the affairs of state. (*He crosses slowly to the throne* C) My legs! My back! This palace is wretchedly heated. Full of draughts and gales.

(*The* GUARD *comes to attention*)

What about those broken window-panes? Have they replaced the tiles on the roof? No-one does any work any more. I shall have to see to it myself, I suppose.

(MARIE *moves to the King to support him*)

You can't count on anyone. (*To Marie*) No, I can manage. (*He helps himself up on to the throne with his sceptre, using it as a stick*) There's some use in this sceptre yet.

(*The* KING *manages to sit, painfully, helped after all by* MARIE)

No, I say, no, I can do it. That's it. There we are.

(MARGUERITE *and* MARIE *sit on their thrones*)

This throne's got very hard. We ought to have it upholstered. And how is my country this morning?

MARGUERITE. What remains of it . . .

KING. There are still a few tidbits left. We've got to keep an eye on them, anyhow. And it'll give you something to think about. Let us send for all our Ministers.

(JULIETTE *enters down* L)

(*To Juliette*) Go and fetch the Ministers. I expect they're still fast asleep.

(*The* GUARD *sniggers*)

They imagine there's no more work to be done.

JULIETTE. They've gone off on their holidays. Not very far, because now the country's all squashed up. It's shrunk. They're at the opposite end of the kingdom; in other words, just round the corner at the edge of the wood beside the stream. They've gone fishing. They hope to catch a few to feed the population.

KING. Fetch them.

JULIETTE. They won't come. They're off duty. But I'll go and see, if you like. (*She goes to the windows and looks out*) They've fallen into the stream.

MARIE. Try and fish them out.

(JULIETTE *exits down* L)

KING. If the country could produce any other political experts, I'd give those two the sack.

MARIE. We'll find some more.

DOCTOR. We won't find any more, Your Majesty.

MARGUERITE. You won't find any more, Berenger.

MARIE. Yes, we will, among the schoolchildren, when they've grown up. We've a little time to wait, but once these two have been fished out, they can keep things going for a while.

DOCTOR. The only children you find in the schools today are a few congenital mental defectives, Mongoloids and hydrocephalics with goitre.

KING. I do see the nation's not very fit. Try and cure them, Doctor, or improve their condition a bit. So, at least, they can learn the first four or five letters of the alphabet. In the old days, we used to kill them off.

DOCTOR. His Majesty could no longer allow himself that privilege, or he'd have no subjects left.

KING. Do something about them, anyway.

MARGUERITE. We can't improve anything, now. We can't cure anyone. Even *you* are incurable, now.

DOCTOR (*crossing behind Marguerite's throne* RC *to* R *of the King*) Sire, you are now incurable.

KING. I am not ill.

MARIE. He feels quite well. (*To the King*) Don't you?

KING. A little stiffness, that's all. It's nothing. It's a lot better now, anyway.

MARIE. He says it's better, you see.

KING. Really, I feel fine.

MARGUERITE. You're going to die in an hour and a half, you're going to die at the end of this show.

KING. What did you say, my dear? That's not very funny.

MARGUERITE. You're going to die at the end of this show.

MARIE. Oh, God!

DOCTOR. Yes, Sire, you are going to die. You will not take your breakfast tomorrow morning. Nor will you dine tonight. The chef has shut off the gas. He's handed in his apron. He's put the table-cloths and napkins away in a cupboard for ever.

MARIE. Don't say it so fast, don't say it so loud.

KING (*rising*) And who can have given such orders, without my consent? I'm in perfectly good health. You're teasing me. It's lies. (*To Marguerite*) You've always wanted me dead. (*To Marie*) She's always wanted me dead. (*To Marguerite*) I'll die when I want to. I'm the King. I'm the one to decide.

DOCTOR. You've lost the power to decide for yourself, Your Majesty.

MARGUERITE. And now you can't even help falling ill.

KING. I'm *not* ill. (*To Marie*) Didn't you say just now I 'wasn't ill? I'm still handsome.

MARGUERITE. And those pains of yours?

KING (*resuming his seat*) All gone.

MARGUERITE. Move about a bit.

(*The* KING *tries to stand, but cannot.* MARIE *gasps.* MARGUERITE *and the* DOCTOR *look at each other*)

KING. That's because I wasn't mentally prepared. You didn't give me time to think. I think and I am cured. A King can cure himself, but I have been too engrossed, ruling my kingdom.

MARGUERITE. Your kingdom! What a state *that's* in. You can't govern it, now. Really, you *know* you can't, but you won't admit it. You've lost your power, now, over yourself and over the elements. You can't stop the rot and you've no more power over us.

MARIE. You'll always have power over me.

MARGUERITE. Not even you.

(JULIETTE *enters down* L. *She carries her broom*)

JULIETTE (*crossing to* LC) It's too late to fish the Ministers out, now.

The stream they fell into, with all its banks and willows, has vanished into a bottomless pit. (*She moves down* L)

KING. I see. It's a plot. You want me to abdicate.

MARGUERITE. That's the best way. A voluntary abdication

DOCTOR. Abdicate, Sire. That would be best.

KING. Abdicate? Me?

MARGUERITE. Yes. Abdicate governmentally. And morally.

DOCTOR. And physically.

MARIE. Don't give your consent. Don't listen to them.

KING. They're mad. Or else they're traitors.

(*The* DOCTOR *crosses to* R)

JULIETTE. Sire, Sire, my poor lord and master, Sire.

MARIE (*rising and moving to* L *of the King*) Have them arrested. (*She holds his hand*)

KING (*to the Guard*) Guard! Arrest them!

(*The* GUARD *crosses to* LC *and turns to face* R)

MARIE. Guard! Arrest them! (*To the King*) That's it. Give orders.

KING. Lock them up in the tower. No, the tower's collapsed. Lock them in the cellar, or in the rabbit hutch. Arrest them, all of them. That's an order.

MARIE (*to the Guard*) Arrest them!

GUARD (*without moving*) In the name of His Majesty—I—I—arrest—you.

MARIE (*moving a little down* LC; *to the Guard*) Get a move on, then.

JULIETTE. He's the one who's arrested.

KING. Do it, then, Guard. Do it!

MARGUERITE. You see, now *he* can't move. He's got gout and rheumatism.

DOCTOR (*indicating the Guard*) Sire, the army is paralysed. An unknown virus has crept into his brain to sabotage his strong points.

MARGUERITE (*to the King*) Your Majesty, you can see for yourself it's your own orders that paralyse him.

MARIE (*moving to* L *of the King*) Don't believe it. She's trying to hypnotize you. It's a question of will-power.

GUARD. I—you—in the name of the King—I—you . . . (*He stops speaking, his mouth wide open*)

KING (*to the Guard*) What's come over you? Speak! Advance! Do you think you're playing statues?

MARIE. Don't ask him questions. Don't argue. Give orders. Sweep him off his feet in a whirlwind of will-power.

DOCTOR. You see, Your Majesty, he can't move a muscle. He can't say a word, he's turned to stone. (*He crosses to* R *of the Guard*) He's deaf to you already. It's a characteristic symptom. Very pronounced, medically speaking. (*He moves to* R *of Marguerite*)

(JULIETTE *prods the Guard with her broom. The* GUARD *crosses to* R *and turns*)

B

MARIE (*to the King*) Prove that you still have power. You can if you want to.

KING. I will prove it.

MARIE. Stand up, first.

KING. I stand up. (*He makes a great effort, grimacing, and rises*)

MARIE. You see how easy it is.

KING (*moving down the steps of the throne*) You see, both of you, how easy it is. You pair of humbugs. Conspirators, Bolsheviks! (*He moves to Marie*)

(MARIE *tries to support him*)

No, no, alone—because I can, by myself. (*He falls and his crown falls off*)

(JULIETTE *rushes forward to pick him up*)

I can get up by myself. (*He rises by himself, but with difficulty*)

(JULIETTE *exits down* L)

GUARD. Long live the King!

(*The* KING *falls down again*)

The King is dying.

MARIE. Long live the King!

(*The* KING, *with difficulty, kneels up*)

GUARD. Long live the King!

(*The* KING *topples sideways*)

The King is dead.

MARIE. Long live the King! Long live the King!

MARGUERITE (*rising*) What a farce!

(*The* KING *stands up, painfully. The following little episode should be played like a tragic Punch and Judy show.*
         JULIETTE *enters up* L)

JULIETTE. Long live the King!

(JULIETTE *disappears behind the throne up* C. *The* KING *falls*)

GUARD. The King is dying!

MARIE. No! Long live the King! Stand up! Long live the King!

(JULIETTE *appears* R *of the throne up* C. *The* KING *rises*)

JULIETTE. Long live the King!

(JULIETTE *exits up* R)

GUARD. Long live the King!

MARIE. You see, he's better now.

MARGUERITE. It's his last burst of energy, isn't it, Doctor?

DOCTOR. Clearly the last burst of energy before his strength gives out.

KING. I tripped, that's all. It could happen to anyone. My crown.

(MARIE *picks up the crown and puts it on the King's head*)

That's a bad omen.

MARIE. Don't you believe it.

(*The* KING *drops his sceptre*)

KING. That's another bad omen.

MARIE (*picking up the sceptre*) Don't believe it. (*She hands the sceptre to the King*) Hold it firmly in your hand. Clench your fist.

GUARD. Long live—long live . . . (*He falls silent*)

DOCTOR (*moving* RC; *to the King*) Your Majesty . . .

MARGUERITE (*moving to* L *of the Doctor and indicating Marie*) We must keep that woman quiet. She says anything that comes into her head. She's not to open her mouth again without our permission. (*She crosses above the King and stands between him and Marie*)

(MARIE *stands motionless*)

(*To the Doctor; indicating the King*) Now, try and make him understand.

DOCTOR (*moving to* R *of the King*) Your Majesty, several decades or even three days ago, your Empire was flourishing. In three days you've lost all the wars you won. And those you lost, you've lost again. And consider—the rockets you want to fire can't even get off the ground. Or else they leave the pad, and drop back to earth with a thud.

KING. A technical hitch.

DOCTOR. There weren't any in the past.

MARGUERITE (*moving down* L *of the King*) Your triumphs are over. You've got to realize that.

DOCTOR. Your pains, your stiffness . . .

KING. I never had them before. This is the first time.

DOCTOR. Exactly. That's the sign. It really has happened all at once, hasn't it?

MARGUERITE. You should have expected it.

DOCTOR. It's happened all at once and you're no longer your own master. You must have noticed, Sire. Try and have the courage to look facts in the face. Just try.

KING. I picked myself up.

DOCTOR. You're a very sick man, and you could never make that effort again.

MARGUERITE. Of course not. It won't be long, now. (*To the King*) What can you still *do?* Can you give an order that's obeyed?

KING. You'll soon see what I can do. Guard, come here.

(*The* GUARD *is motionless. The* DOCTOR *moves a little up* R *of the King*)

MARGUERITE. He can't. He can only obey other people, now. Guard, two paces forward.

(*The* GUARD *advances two paces*)

Guard, two paces back.

(*The* GUARD *retires two paces*)

KING. Off with that Guard's head, off with his head.

(*The* GUARD's *head leans a little to the right, then a little to the left*)

His head's toppling. It's going to fall.

MARGUERITE. No, it isn't. It wobbles a bit, that's all.

(*The* DOCTOR *moves to* R *of the King*)

KING. Off with that Doctor's head, off with it at once.

MARGUERITE. The Doctor has a sound head on his shoulders. He's got it screwed on all right.

DOCTOR. I'm sorry, Sire; as you see, I feel quite ashamed.

KING. Off with Marguerite's crown. Knock it off. (*He brandishes his sceptre and accidentally knocks his own crown off*)

(*The* DOCTOR *moves a little* R)

MARGUERITE (*crossing above the King to* R *of him*) All right, I'll put it on again. (*She picks up the crown, puts it on the King's head then moves to* L *of the Doctor*)

KING. Thank you. What *is* all this? Witchcraft? How have I lost my power over you? (*He crosses to* L) Don't imagine I'm going to let things go on like this. I'm going to get to the bottom of this. There must be rust in the machine. (*He moves up* C) It stops the wheels from turning.

MARGUERITE (*to Marie*) You can speak, now. We give you permission.

MARIE (*to the King*) Tell me to do something and I'll do it. Give me an order. Command me, Sire, command me. I'll obey you.

MARGUERITE (*to the Doctor*) She thinks what she calls love can achieve the impossible. Sentimental superstition. Things have changed. That's out of the question, now. We're past that stage already.

MARIE (*backing down* L) Order me, my King. Order me, my love. See how beautiful I am. Smell my perfume. Order me to come to you, to kiss you.

KING. Come to me—kiss me.

(MARIE *does not move*)

Can you hear me?

MARIE. Why, yes, I can hear you. I'll do it.

KING. Come on, then.

MARIE. I'd like to. I'm going to. I want to do it. But my arms fall to my side.

KING. Dance, then.

(MARIE *does not move*)

Dance! Or turn your head.

MARIE. I can't.

KING. I expect you've got a stiff neck. You must have a stiff neck. (*He takes a step or two towards Marie*) Come closer to me.

MARIE. Yes, Sire.

KING. And smile.

MARIE. Yes, Sire.

KING. Do it, then.

MARIE. I don't know what to do, how to walk. I've suddenly forgotten.

MARGUERITE (*to Marie*) Take a few steps nearer.

(MARIE *slowly advances a little in the direction of the King*)

KING. You see, she's coming.

MARGUERITE. Because she listened to *me*. (*To Marie*) Stop! Stand still.

(MARIE *stops*)

MARIE (*to the King*) Forgive me, Your Majesty. It's not my fault.

MARGUERITE (*moving to* R *of the King*) Do you need more proof?

(*The* KING *moves to the throne up* C. MARGUERITE *moves to* R *of the King. The* DOCTOR *moves to* R *of Marguerite*)

KING. I order trees to sprout from the floor. (*He pauses*) I order the roof to disappear. (*He pauses*) What? Nothing? (*He pauses and sits on his throne*) I order a thunderbolt, one I can hold in my hand. (*He pauses*) Nothing? I order Juliette to come in through the great door.

(*They all look towards the door down* R.
JULIETTE *enters down* L *and crosses to the door down* R)

I order you to stay.

(JULIETTE *exits down* R)

I order bugles to sound, bells to ring. (*He rises*) A salute from a hundred and twenty-one guns in my honour. (*He listens*) Nothing. Wait! Yes! I can hear something.

DOCTOR. It's only the buzzing in your ears, Your Majesty.

MARGUERITE (*moving to her throne* RC) Don't try any more. (*She sits*) You're making a fool of yourself.

(MARIE *moves to the King and sits him on his throne. The* DOCTOR *moves up* R)

MARIE. You're—you're getting tired, my dear little King. Don't

despair. You're soaked in perspiration. Rest a little. After a while,
we'll start again. Wait for an hour and then we'll manage it.

MARGUERITE (*to the King*) In one hour and twenty-five minutes,
you're going to die.

DOCTOR (*moving to* R *of Marguerite and looking at his watch*) Yes, Sire.
In one hour, twenty-four minutes and fifty seconds.

KING. Marie!

MARGUERITE. In one hour, twenty-four minutes and forty-one
seconds. Prepare yourself.

MARIE (*to the King*) Don't give in.

MARGUERITE (*rising*) Stop trying to distract him. You can't hold
him back, now. The official programme must be followed stage by
stage. (*She signals to the Guard*)

(*The* GUARD *faces front*)

GUARD (*announcing*) The ceremony is about to commence. (*He
turns and faces* L)

(*There is general commotion. They all take up their positions as if for
some solemn ceremony.* MARGUERITE *and* MARIE *sit on their thrones.*

JULIETTE *enters down* R, *goes in turn to Marguerite and Marie and
spreads out their trains. The* KING *is seated on his throne* C. *The* DOCTOR
stands R *of Marguerite.* JULIETTE *finishes with the trains and stands* L)

KING. Let time turn back in its tracks.

MARIE. Let us be as we were twenty years ago.

KING. Let it be last week.

MARIE. Let it be yesterday evening. Turn back, time. Turn back!
Time, stop!

(*The* DOCTOR *raises his telescope and looks heavenwards through it*)

MARGUERITE. There is no more time. Time has melted in his
hands.

(*The* KING *sinks down in his throne*)

DOCTOR (*lowering his telescope*) If you look through this telescope—

(*The* KING *slips down on to the steps of the throne*)

—which can see through roofs and walls, you will notice a gap in
the sky that used to house the Royal Constellation. In the annals of
the Universe, his Majesty has been entered as deceased. (*He snaps his
telescope shut*)

GUARD. The King is dead! Long live the King!

MARGUERITE (*to the Guard*) Idiot! Be quiet!

DOCTOR. He is, indeed, far more dead than alive.

KING. I'm not. I don't want to die. Please don't let me die. I
don't want to, I don't want to.

DOCTOR. The crisis I was expecting. It's perfectly normal. The
first breach in his defences, already.

(MARGUERITE *and* MARIE *rise*)

MARGUERITE (*to Marie*) The crisis will pass.
GUARD. The King is passing.
DOCTOR (*crossing to* R *of the King*) We shall miss your Majesty greatly. And we shall say so publicly. That's a promise.
KING. Don't want.
MARIE. Oh, look! His hair has suddenly gone white.

(*The* KING's *hair has indeed turned white*)

The wrinkles are spreading across his forehead, over his face. (*She crosses above the throne* RC *to* R *of it*) All at once, he looks fourteen centuries older.

(JULIETTE *approaches the King, looks at him, then backs up* R *of the throne* LC)

DOCTOR. Antiquated. And so suddenly, too.
KING. Kings ought to be immortal.
MARGUERITE. They are. Provisionally.
KING. They promised me *I* could choose the time when I would die.

(*The* DOCTOR *crosses to* R)

MARGUERITE (*moving to* R *of the King*) That's because they thought you'd have chosen long ago. But you acquired a taste for authority. Now you must be *made* to choose. You got stuck in the mud of life. You felt warm and cosy. (*Sharply*) Now you're going to freeze.
KING. I've been trapped. I should have been warned.
MARGUERITE. You were often warned.
KING. You warned me too soon. (*He tries to rise*) Someone must save me, I can't save myself.
MARGUERITE. You'd been condemned, and you should have thought about that the very first day, and then day after day, five minutes every day. It wasn't much to give up. Five minutes every day. Then ten minutes, a quarter, half an hour. That's the way to train yourself.
KING. I *did* think about it.
MARGUERITE. Not seriously, not profoundly, never with all your heart and soul.
MARIE (*crossing to the foot of the throne* LC) He was so alive.
MARGUERITE. Too much alive. (*To the King*) You ought to have had this thought permanently at the back of your mind.
DOCTOR. He never looked ahead, he's always lived from day to day, like most people.
MARGUERITE. You kept on putting it off. At twenty you said you'd wait till your fortieth year before you went into training. At forty . . .
KING. I was in such good health, I was so young.

MARGUERITE. At forty: why not wait until you were fifty? At fifty . . .

KING. I was full of life, wonderfully full of life.

MARGUERITE. At fifty, you wanted first to reach your sixties. And so you went on, from sixty to ninety to a hundred and twenty-five to two hundred, until you were four hundred years old. Instead of putting things off for ten years at a time, you put them off for fifty. Then you postponed them from century to century.

KING. But I was just about to start. If only I could have a whole century before me.

DOCTOR. All you have now is one hour, Sire. You must do it all in an hour.

MARIE. He'll never have enough time, it's impossible. He must be given more.

MARGUERITE. *That* is impossible. But an hour gives him all the time he needs.

DOCTOR. A well-spent hour's better than whole centuries of neglect and failure. Five minutes are enough, ten fully conscious seconds. We're giving him an hour. Sixty minutes, three thousand and six hundred seconds. He's in luck.

MARGUERITE (*sitting on her throne*) He's lingered too long by the wayside.

JULIETTE (*moving to R of Marie*) Poor Majesty, my poor master's been playing truant.

KING. I'm like a schoolboy who hasn't done his homework, sitting for an exam. What a state I'm in.

GUARD (*announcing*) The King has just alluded to his state.

MARGUERITE. A state of ignorance.

JULIETTE. He'd like to go on playing truant for centuries to come.

KING. I'd like to re-sit the exam.

MARGUERITE. No re-sits are allowed. You'll take it now. (*She looks at the Doctor*)

DOCTOR. There's nothing you can do, Your Majesty. Neither can we. We only practise medical science, we can't perform miracles.

KING. Do the people know? (*He rises with difficulty*) Have you warned them? I want everyone to know that the King is going to die. (*He makes a rush to the window, with a great effort, for his limp is getting worse. He opens the window and speaks out of it*) My good people, I am going to die.

MARGUERITE (*rising; to the Doctor*) They mustn't hear him. Stop him shouting.

(*The* DOCTOR *crosses to the King.* JULIETTE *and* MARIE *move slightly* C)

KING (*shouting*) Your King is going to die! Hands off the King! I want the whole world to know. I'm going to die.

DOCTOR. Scandalous!

KING. My people, I've got to die.

MARGUERITE (*moving down* RC) What was once a king is now a pig that's being slaughtered.

MARIE. He's just a king. He's just a man.

DOCTOR. Your Majesty, think of the death of Louis the Fourteenth, of Philip the Second, or of the Emperor Charles the Fifth who slept in his own coffin for twenty years. It is your Majesty's duty to die with dignity.

KING. With dignity? (*Through the window*) Help! Your King is going to die.

MARIE. My poor dear King, my poor little King.

JULIETTE. Shouting won't help.

(*A feeble echo can be heard in the distance: "The King is going to die"*)

KING. Hear that?

MARIE. *I* hear, *I* can hear.

KING. They've answered me. (*He crosses to* R) Perhaps they're going to save me.

JULIETTE. There's no-one there.

(*The echo can be heard: "Help!"*)

DOCTOR. It's only the echo, a bit late in answering.

MARGUERITE. Late as usual, like everything else in this country.

KING. It's impossible. (*He crosses to the window*) It's impossible.

MARGUERITE. He imagines no-one's ever died before.

MARIE. No-one *has* died before.

MARGUERITE. It's all very painful.

JULIETTE. He's crying. Just like anyone else.

MARGUERITE. Terror only makes him banal. I hoped it would inspire him to something worth recording. We'll have to borrow some famous last words—we'll invent some, if need be.

DOCTOR. We'll credit him with some edifying maxims. (*To Marguerite*) We'll watch over his legend. (*To the King*) We'll watch over your legend, Your Majesty.

KING (*at the window*) People, help! Help, people!

MARGUERITE. Haven't you had enough, Your Majesty? It's a waste of effort.

KING (*at the window*) Who will give me his life? Who will give his life for the King's? His life for the good old King's, his life for the poor old King's?

MARGUERITE. It's indecent.

MARIE. Give him every possible chance.

JULIETTE. As there's no-one left in the country to hear, why not?

(JULIETTE *exits down* L)

DOCTOR. The echo's stopped answering. His voice doesn't carry any more. (*He moves to* R *of Marguerite*) He can shout as much as he likes. It won't even reach as far as the garden wall.

MARGUERITE. He's moaning.
DOCTOR. We're the only ones who can hear him, now. He can't even hear himself.

(*The* KING *turns from the window and moves* C)

MARIE. His legs are all stiff.
DOCTOR. He's riddled with rheumatism. (*To Marguerite*) An injection to quieten him?

(JULIETTE *enters up* LC *pushing a wheel-chair which has a crown and royal emblems on the back. On the chair there is a blanket, a hot-water bottle and the King's nightcap*)

KING (*moving up* L *of Marie*) I won't have an injection.
MARIE (*moving to* R *of the King*) No injection.
KING. I know what they mean. I've had injections given to other people. (*To Juliette*) I never told you to bring that chair. (*He crosses towards the door down* R) I'm going for a walk. I wish to take the air.

(JULIETTE *puts the wheel-chair down* L)

MARGUERITE. Sit down in that chair or you'll fall.

(*The* KING *is, in fact, staggering*)

KING. I intend to stay on my feet.
JULIETTE. You'd feel much better, Sire, much more comfortable with a blanket over your knees and a hot-water bottle.
KING. No. I want—I want to scream. (*He screams*)
GUARD (*announcing*) His Majesty is screaming.
DOCTOR (*to Marguerite*) He won't scream for long. I know the symptoms. He'll get tired. He'll stop and then he'll listen to us.

(JULIETTE *picks up the blanket and hot-water bottle from the wheel-chair*)

KING (*to Juliette*) Take them away.
MARGUERITE. Sit down quickly, sit down.
KING (*moving to his throne*) I refuse. (*He tries to climb the steps of the throne and fails*)

(*The* DOCTOR, MARGUERITE *and* MARIE *move to the King to help him. The* KING *staggers. The* DOCTOR *and* MARGUERITE *help the* KING *to sit on the throne* RC, *where he collapses*)

I nearly fell over. Me!

(JULIETTE *replaces the blanket and hot-water bottle in the wheel-chair and picks up the nightcap*)

MARGUERITE (*to Juliette*) Take his sceptre, it's too heavy for him. (*She removes the King's crown*)

(JULIETTE *takes the nightcap to the King*)

KING (*to Juliette*) I won't wear that.

JULIETTE. It's a sort of crown, but not so heavy. (*She puts the cap on the King's head and grasps the sceptre*)

KING. Let me keep my sceptre.

MARGUERITE. You've no longer the strength to hold it.

(JULIETTE *takes the sceptre from the King, then takes the crown from Marguerite and puts it under the King's throne*)

DOCTOR. It's no good trying to lean on it, now. We'll carry you. We'll wheel you along in that chair.

KING. I want to keep it.

MARIE (*to Juliette*) Let him have his sceptre back. He wants it.

(JULIETTE *looks to Marguerite for her instructions*)

MARGUERITE. Very well, I don't see why not.

(JULIETTE *returns the sceptre to the King then moves* L)

KING. Perhaps it's not true. Tell me it's not true. Perhaps it's a nightmare.

(*The others are silent*)

Perhaps there's a ten to one chance, one chance in a thousand. (*He sobs*)

(*The others are silent*)

I often used to win the sweepstake.

DOCTOR. Your Majesty!

KING. I won't hear any more talk, your words scare me. (*He sobs and moans*)

MARGUERITE. You must listen, Sire.

KING. I can't listen to you any more, I'm too frightened.

(MARIE *moves towards the King*)

Don't you come any nearer, either. You scare me with your pity.

MARIE (*moving a little down* LC) He's like a small child—a little boy again.

MARGUERITE. An ugly little boy, with wrinkles.

JULIETTE. You try and put yourself in his place. (*She moves* L)

KING (*rising painfully*) Speak to me! (*He moves towards the throne* LC) I didn't mean it, speak to me.

(MARIE *moves to* R *of the King,* JULIETTE *to* L *of him and they assist him to sit on the throne* LC)

Stand by me, hold me. Help me up. I want to run away.

(MARIE *stands* R *of the King and* JULIETTE L *of him.* MARGUERITE *moves to* L *of the throne* RC *and the* DOCTOR *to* R *of the throne* RC)

JULIETTE. His legs can hardly carry him.

KING. It hurts to move my arms, too. Does that mean it's starting? Why was I born if it wasn't for ever? Damn my parents! What a joke, what a farce. I came into the world five minutes ago. I got married three minutes ago.

MARGUERITE. Two hundred and eighty-three years.

KING. I came to the throne two and a half minutes ago.

MARGUERITE. Two hundred and seventy-seven years and three months.

KING. Never had time to say "Jack Robinson".

MARGUERITE. He never even tried. (*She moves down* R. *To the Doctor*) Yet he had the greatest experts to tell him all about it. Theologians, people of experience, and books he never read.

KING. I never had the time.

MARGUERITE. You used to say you had all the time in the world.

KING. I never had the time, I never had the time, I never had the time.

JULIETTE. He's going back to that again. (*She moves to the wheelchair*)

DOCTOR (*moving to* L *of Marguerite*) I'd say things were looking up. (*He looks at the King*) However much he moans and groans, he started to reason things out. (*He turns to Marguerite*) He's complaining, protesting. That means he's begun to resign himself.

KING. I shall never resign myself.

DOCTOR. As he says he won't, it's a sign that he *will*. He's posing the problem of resignation, raising the question.

MARGUERITE (*crossing down* L *of the King*) At last.

DOCTOR. Your Majesty, you have made war one hundred and eighty times. You have led your armies into two thousand battles. First, on a white horse with a conspicuous red and white plume. Then, when you modernized the army, you would stand on top of a tank, or on the wing of a fighter plane, leading the formation. You never knew fear.

MARIE. He was a hero.

DOCTOR. You have come near death a thousand times.

KING. I only came *near* it. I knew it wasn't meant for me.

MARIE (*moving up* R *of the throne* LC) You were a hero. Remember that.

MARGUERITE (*moving* C) Aided and abetted by this doctor, this executioner here, you ordered the assassination.

KING. Execution, not assassination.

DOCTOR (*to Marguerite*) Execution, Your Majesty, not assassination. I was only obeying orders. I was a mere instrument, just an executor, not an executioner. It was all euthanasia to me. Anyhow, I'm sorry. Please forgive me.

MARGUERITE (*moving to* R *of the King*) I tell you, you had my parents butchered, your own brothers, your rivals, our cousins and great grand cousins, and all their families, friends and cattle. You massacred the lot and scorched all their lands.

DOCTOR. His Majesty used to say they were going to die one day, anyway.

KING. That was for reasons of State.

MARGUERITE (*moving to the throne* RC) You're dying, too, because of your state. (*She sits*)

KING. But I *am* the State.

JULIETTE. And what a state the poor man's in.

MARIE. He was the law, above the law.

KING (*groaning*) I'm not above the law any more.

GUARD (*announcing*) The King is no more above the law.

(*The* KING *rises, moves painfully to the throne* C, *gives his sceptre to* JULIETTE, *who puts it with the crown, then sits on the steps of the throne*)

JULIETTE. The poor old boy's no more above the law. He's just like us and not unlike my granddad.

MARIE (*moving to* L *of the King*) Poor little chap, poor child.

KING. Child! A child? Then I can make a fresh start. I want to start again. (*To Marie*) I want to be a baby and you can be my mother.

(MARIE *sits on the throne* LC)

Then they won't come for me. I still don't know my reading, writing, and arithmetic. What do two and two make?

JULIETTE. Two and two make four.

MARGUERITE (*to the King*) You knew that already.

KING. Oh, dear, it's no good trying to cheat. There are so many people being born at this moment, numberless babies all over the world.

MARGUERITE. Not in *our* country.

DOCTOR. The birth-rate's down to zero. (*He crosses above the throne* LC *to* L *of Marguerite*)

JULIETTE. Not a lettuce grows, not a blade of grass. Perhaps one day everything will grow again.

MARGUERITE. When he's accepted the inevitable. When he's gone.

KING. When I've gone, when I've gone. They'll laugh and stuff themselves silly and dance on my tomb. As if I'd never existed. Oh, please make them all remember me. (*He rises*) Make everyone learn my life by heart. Let the schoolchildren and the scholars study nothing else but me, my kingdom and my exploits. (*He moves* RC) Destroy all existing statues and set up mine in all the public squares. My portrait in every Ministry, my photograph in every office of every town hall. (*He crosses to* LC) Let every car and push-cart, flying ship and steamplane be named after me. Make them forget all other captains and kings, poets, tenors and philosophers, and fill every conscious mind with memories of me. Let them learn to read by spelling out my name: B—E—for "Berenger". Let my likeness be on all the ikons, me on the millions of crucifixes in all our churches. Make them say Mass for me and let *me* be the Host. Let all the windows light up in the shape and colour of my eyes. And the rivers trace my profile on the plains. Let them cry my name throughout eternity, and beg me and implore me.

MARIE (*rising and moving to* L *of the King*) Perhaps you'll come back again?

KING. Perhaps I will come back. Let them preserve my body in some palace, on a throne, and let food be put before me. Let musicians play and virgins grovel at my ice-cold feet.

JULIETTE (*to Marguerite*) He's raving, ma'am.

GUARD (*announcing*) His Majesty the King is delirious.

(*The* DOCTOR *crosses to* R *of the King*)

MARGUERITE. Not yet. There's too much sense in what he says. Too much, and not enough.

DOCTOR (*to the King*) If such be your will, Your Majesty, we will embalm your body and preserve it.

JULIETTE. As long as we can.

KING (*sitting on the steps of his throne*) No, no embalming. And I don't want to be burnt. You're not to bury me or throw me to the vultures. I want to feel arms around me, warm arms, cool arms, soft arms, strong arms.

JULIETTE. He's not too sure what he *does* want. (*She weeps*)

MARGUERITE. We'll make his mind up for him. (*To Marie*) Now, don't faint. (*She points to Juliette*) And there's another one. What a pair!

KING. If I *am* remembered, let them remember me to the end of time. And beyond the end of time, in twenty thousand years, in two hundred and fifty-five thousand million years . . . They'll forget long before that. Selfish, the lot of them. They only think of their own little lives, of their own skins. Not of *mine*. If the whole earth's going to explode, explode it will. It's all the same whether it's tomorrow or in countless centuries to come. What's got to finish one day is finished now.

MARGUERITE. Everything is yesterday.

JULIETTE. Even "today" will be "yesterday".

DOCTOR. All things pass into the past.

MARIE (*moving to* L *of the King*) My darling King, there is no past, there is no future. Remember, there's only a present that goes right on to the end, everything is present. Be present, be the present.

KING. Alas! I'm only present in the past.

MARGUERITE. That's right, Berenger, try and get things straight.

MARIE. Yes, my King, get things straight, my darling. Stop torturing yourself. (*She sits* L *of the King on the steps*) Remember, I implore you to remember that morning in June we spent together by the sea, when happiness raced through you and inflamed you. You knew then what joy meant—you felt it—rich, changeless and undying love. You found that fiery radiance within you. If it was there once, it is still there, now. Find that radiance again—look for it—in yourself.

KING. I don't understand.

MARIE. You don't understand yourself any more.

MARGUERITE. He never did understand himself.

MARIE (*rising*) Pull yourself together, I implore you.

KING. How do I manage that? (*He moves himself on to a higher step*)

(MARIE *moves* LC)

No-one can or will help me. And *I* can't help myself. Oh, help me, sun. Sun, chase away these shadows and hold back the night. Sun, sun, light up every tomb, shine into every hole and corner, nook and cranny. Creep deep inside me. Ah! My feet are turning cold. Sun, will you miss me? Good little sun, protect me. And if you're in need of some small sacrifice, then parch and wither up the world. Let every human creature die provided *I* can live for ever, even alone in a limitless desert. I'll come to terms with solitude. I'll keep alive the memory of others, and I'll miss them quite sincerely. It's better to miss one's friends than to be missed oneself. Sun, sun, let me go on living, century after century, even with raging toothache. But I fear what must end one day has ended now.

DOCTOR. Well, Sire, what are you waiting for?

MARGUERITE. It's only his speeches that are never-ending. (*She indicates Marie and Juliette*) And these two weeping women. They only push him deeper in the mire, trap him, bind him and hold him up.

KING. No, there's not enough weeping. (*To Marguerite*) Don't stop them weeping for their king, their young king, old king, poor little king. *I* feel pity when I think how they'll miss me, never see me again. I'm still the one who thinks about others. (*He sobs*) I'm dying, I keep trying to tell you. I'm dying, but I can't express it, unless I talk like a book and make literature of it.

DOCTOR. And that's the way it goes on, to the bitter end. As long as we live we turn everything into literature.

MARIE. If only it could console him.

GUARD (*announcing*) The King finds some consolation in literature.

KING. No, no. Nothing can console me. It just wells up inside me, then drains away again. Oh, dear, oh, dear, oh, dear, oh, dear, oh, dear. (*Lamentations, then without declamation, he goes on moaning gently to himself*) Help me, you countless thousands who died before me. Tell me how you managed to accept death. Teach me. Let me lean on you like crutches. Help me to cross the threshold you have crossed. Come back from the other side and help me. Help me, you who were frightened and did not want to go. What was it like? Who held you up? Who dragged you there, who pushed you? Were you afraid to the very end? And you who were strong and courageous, who

accepted death with indifference and serenity, teach me your indifference and serenity, teach me resignation.

(*The following dialogue should be spoken and acted as though it were
ritual, with solemnity, almost chanted, accompanied by various movements,
with the actors kneeling, holding their arms, etc.*)

JULIETTE (*kneeling*) You statues, you dark or shining phantoms,
ancients, and shades . . .

MARIE (*kneeling*) Teach him serenity.

GUARD (*kneeling*) Teach him indifference.

DOCTOR. Teach him resignation.

MARGUERITE (*rising*) Make him see reason and set his mind at rest.

(*The* KING *rises, moves* c *and kneels*)

KING. You suicides, teach me how to feel disgust for life. Teach
me lassitude. What drug must I take for that?

DOCTOR. I could prescribe euphoric pills or tranquillizers.

MARGUERITE. He'd vomit them up.

JULIETTE. You remembrances . . .

GUARD. You pictures of days gone by . . .

JULIETTE. —which no longer exist but in our memories of
memories . . .

GUARD. Recollections of recollections——

MARGUERITE. He's got to learn to let go and then surrender completely.

GUARD (*raising his arm*) —we invoke you.

MARIE. You morning mists and dews——

JULIETTE. You evening smoke and clouds——

MARIE. —you saints, you wise and foolish virgins, help him. For *I*
cannot.

JULIETTE. —help him.

KING. You who died happy, who looked death in the face, who
remained conscious of your end—help me.

JULIETTE. Help him.

MARIE. Help him, all of you. Help him, I beg you.

KING. You who died blissfully, what face did you see close to
yours? What smile gave you ease and made *you* smile? What were
the last rays of light that brushed your face?

JULIETTE. Help him, you thousand millions of the dead.

GUARD. Oh, you, great Nothing, help the King.

KING. I am the dying agony of all. So many worlds will flicker
out in me.

MARGUERITE (*moving above the King*) Life is exile.

KING. But I like being in exile.

DOCTOR. In short, Majesty, you will return to your own country.

MARIE. You'll go back where you came from when you were
born. Don't be so frightened, you're sure to find something familiar
there.

KING. When faced with death, even a tiny ant puts up a fight. In him, too, the universe flickers out. It's not natural to die, because no-one ever wants to. I want to exist.

(*The* KING, MARIE, JULIETTE *and the* GUARD *rise*)

JULIETTE. That's all he knows. He wants to exist for ever.

KING. Doctor, Doctor, am I in the throes of death already? No, you've made a mistake. Not yet. Not yet. (*He gives a kind of sigh of relief*) It hasn't started yet. I exist, I'm still here. I can see. There are walls and furniture here, and air to breathe. I can think, I can see, I can hear. A fanfare!

(*A sort of fanfare can be heard far away in the distance. The* KING *moves towards the throne*)

GUARD. The King is walking. Long live the King!

(*The* KING *falls down*)

JULIETTE. He's down.
GUARD. The King is down. The King is dying.

(*The* KING *rises*)

MARIE. He's up again.
GUARD. The King is up. Long live the King.
MARIE. He's up again.
GUARD. Long live the King!

(*The* KING *falls down*)

The King is dead.

(*The* KING *rises*)

MARIE. He's still alive. He's up again.
GUARD. Long live the King.

(*The* KING *moves to his throne*)

JULIETTE. He wants to sit on his throne.
MARIE. The King still reigns. The King still reigns.

(JULIETTE *moves to the King and helps him*)

DOCTOR. And now for the delirium.

(*The* KING, *helped by* JULIETTE, *tries to totter up the steps of his throne*)

MARIE. Don't let go, hang on. (*To Juliette*) Leave him alone. He can do it alone.

(*The* KING *fails to climb the steps of the throne.* JULIETTE *crosses to the wheel-chair and moves it* C)

MARGUERITE. We've got thirty-two minutes and thirty seconds left.

C

KING. I can still stand up.

(JULIETTE *goes to the* KING *and helps him to the wheel-chair*)

DOCTOR (*to Marguerite*) It's the last convulsion but one.

(*The* KING *falls into the wheel-chair.* MARIE *collects the sceptre and puts it in the bag hanging on the chair*)

KING. I can still stand up.
MARIE. You're out of breath, you're tired. Have a rest and you can stand up again later.

(JULIETTE *and* MARIE *put the rug around the King and the hot-water bottle behind him*)

MARGUERITE (*to Marie*) Don't lie. That doesn't help him.
KING. I used to like Mozart. I'll never hear his music again.
MARGUERITE. You'll forget all about it.

(MARIE *stands* L *of the King and* JULIETTE *stands* R *of him.* MARGUERITE *is up* R *of Juliette. The* DOCTOR *moves down* R)

KING (*to Juliette*) Did you mend my trousers? Or did you think it not worth the trouble, now? There was a hole in my purple cloak. Have you patched it? Have you sewn those buttons on my other pyjamas? Have you had my shoes re-soled?
JULIETTE. I never gave it another thought.
KING. You never gave it another thought. What *do* you think about? Talk to me. What does your husband do?
JULIETTE. I'm a widow.
KING. What do you think about when you do the housework?
JULIETTE. Nothing, Your Majesty.
KING. What's your family? Where do you come from?
MARGUERITE (*to the King*) You never took any interest before. (*She moves to her throne and sits*)
MARIE. He's never had time to ask her. (*She moves to her throne and sits*)
MARGUERITE (*to the King*) And you're not really interested, now.
DOCTOR. He wants to gain time. (*He moves to* R *of the throne* RC)
KING (*to Juliette*) Tell me, what sort of life do you lead?
JULIETTE. A bad life, Sire. (*She takes out a needle and thread, kneels beside the King and sews his cloak*)
KING. Life can never be bad. That's a contradiction in terms.
JULIETTE. Life's not very beautiful.
KING. Life is life.
JULIETTE. When I get up in the winter, it's still dark. And I'm as cold as ice.
KING. You don't like the cold?
JULIETTE. When I get up in the summer, it's only just beginning to get light. A pale sort of light.

KING (*rapturously*) A *pale* light. There are all sorts of light: blue and pink and white and green, and *pale*.

JULIETTE. I do all the palace laundry in the wash-house. It hurts my hands and cracks my skin.

KING (*rapturously*) And it hurts. You can feel your skin. Haven't they bought you a washing-machine, yet? Marguerite! A palace, and no washing-machine.

MARGUERITE. We had to pawn it to raise a State loan.

KING. Ah, ha!

JULIETTE. I empty the chamber pots. I make the beds.

KING. She makes the beds. Where we lie down and go to sleep and then wake up again. To wake up every day. Every morning one comes into the world.

JULIETTE. I polish the parquet floors, and sweep, sweep, sweep! There's no end to it.

KING (*rapturously*) There's no end to it.

JULIETTE. It gives me the backache. (*She finishes sewing*)

KING. That's right. She has a back. We've all got backs.

JULIETTE. Pains in the kidneys.

KING. And kidneys, too.

JULIETTE. And now we've no gardeners left, I dig and rake and sow.

KING. And then things grow.

JULIETTE. I get quite worn out, exhausted.

KING. You ought to have told me.

JULIETTE. I *did* tell you.

KING. Maybe. Such a lot has escaped my notice.

JULIETTE. There's no window in my room.

KING (*rapturously*) No window! You go out in search of the light. You find it and then you smile. Where do you live?

JULIETTE. In the attic.

KING. To come down in the morning, you take the stairs, you go down one step, then another, down a step, down a step, down a step. And when you get dressed, you put on first your stockings, then your shoes.

JULIETTE. Down at heel.

KING. And a dress. It's amazing.

JULIETTE. A cheap one. A rotten old thing.

KING. A rotten old dress! You don't know what you're saying. It's beautiful.

JULIETTE. Once I had an abscess in my mouth and they pulled out one of my teeth.

KING. You're in terrible pain. But it starts to ease off, and then disappears. It's a tremendous relief that makes you feel wonderfully happy.

JULIETTE. I feel tired, tired, tired.

KING. So you take a rest. That's good.

JULIETTE. Not enough time off for that.

KING. You can still hope you'll have enough time, one day. You go out with a basket and do the shopping. You say "good day" to the grocer.

JULIETTE. He's enormous. Hideously fat. So ugly he frightens the birds and the cats away.

KING. Marvellous! You take out your purse, you pay, and get your change. The market's a medley of green lettuce, red cherries, golden grapes and purple eggplants—all the colours of the rainbow. It's fantastic! Incredible! Like a fairy-tale.

JULIETTE. And then I go home—the same way I came.

KING. You take the same road twice a day. With the sky above you. You can gaze at it twice a day. And you breathe the air. You never realize you're breathing. Think about it. It's a miracle.

JULIETTE. And then, then I have the washing-up from the night before. Plates smothered in sticky fat. And then I have to do the cooking.

KING. Sublime!

JULIETTE. You're wrong. It's boring. It makes me sick.

KING. Some people one will never understand. It's wonderful to feel bored and *not* to feel bored, too, to lose one's temper, and to keep one's temper. To practise resignation and to insist on your rights. You get excited, you talk to people and people talk to you, you touch them and they touch you. All this is magical, like some endless celebration.

JULIETTE. You're right there. There's no end to it. (*She rises*) After that, I still have to wait at table.

KING (*rapturously*) You wait at table. You wait at table. What do you serve at table?

JULIETTE. The meal I've just prepared.

KING. What, for example?

JULIETTE. I don't know, the main dish. Stew.

KING (*dreamily*) Stew! Stew!

JULIETTE. It's a meal in itself.

KING. I used to be so fond of stew, with vegetables and potatoes, cabbage and carrots all mixed up with butter, crushed with a fork and mashed together.

JULIETTE. We could bring him some.

KING. Send for some stew.

MARGUERITE (*rising*) No.

JULIETTE. But if he likes it.

DOCTOR. Bad for his health. He's on a diet.

KING. I want some stew.

DOCTOR. It's not what the doctor orders for a dying man.

MARIE (*rising*) But if it's his last wish . . .

MARGUERITE. He must detach himself.

KING. Gravy—hot potatoes—and carrots to lead me by the nose.

JULIETTE (*moving above the King*) He's still making jokes.

KING. It never struck me before how beautiful carrots are. Quick! Go and kill the two spiders in my bedroom. I don't want them to survive me. No, don't kill them. Perhaps in *them* there's something still of *me*. That stew—it's dead. There never was such a thing as stew.

GUARD (*announcing*) Stew has been banished from the length and breadth of the land.

MARGUERITE. At last, something achieved. At least he's given *that* up. Of all the things we crave for, the minor ones go first. Now we can begin. Gently, as you remove a dressing from an open sore, first lifting the corners, because they're farthest from the centre of the wound.

(JULIETTE *puts on a nurse's white cap and apron*)

(*She moves up* R *of the King*) Juliette, wipe the sweat from his face, he's dripping wet.

(MARIE *moves to* L *of the King*)

DOCTOR (*to Marie*) No, not you. (*To Marguerite*) It's panic oozing out through his pores. (*He moves down* R *of the King and examines him for a moment*)

(MARIE *kneels* L *of the King and covers her face with her hands.* JULIETTE, *using a tissue, leans over and wipes the King's face*)

You see, his temperature's gone down, though there's not much sign of gooseflesh. His hair was standing on end before. Now it's lying flat. He's not used to being so terrified, yet, oh, no. But now he can see the fear inside him; that's why he's dared to close his eyes. He'll open them again. He still looks tense, but see how the wrinkles of old age are settling on his face. Already he's letting things take their course. He'll still have a few setbacks. It's not as quick as all that. But he won't have the wind up, any more. That would have been too degrading. (*He suddenly claps his hands*)

(*The* KING's *hands shoot out*)

He'll still be subject to fright, but pure fright, without abdominal complications. We can't hope his death will be an example to others. But it will be fairly respectable. His *death* will kill him, now, and not his fear. We'll have to help him, all the same, Your Majesty —he'll need a lot of help, till the very last second—(*he moves a little* R) till he's drawn his very last breath.

MARGUERITE (*moving to* R *of the King*) I'll help him. I'll drive it out of him. I'll cut him loose. I'll untie every knot and ravel out the tangled skein. I'll separate the wheat from the tenacious tares that cling to him and bind him.

DOCTOR. It won't be easy.

MARIE (*to the King*) Until Death comes, you are still *here*. When Death is here, *you* will have gone. You won't meet her or see her.

MARGUERITE. The lies of life, those old fallacies. Death has always been here, present in the seed since the very first day. (*To*

Marie) Neither your charm nor your charms can bewitch the King any more.

(MARIE *rises*)

GUARD (*announcing*) The charm of Queen Marie no longer casts its spell over the King.

MARIE (*to the King*) You used to love me, you love me still, as I have always loved you.

KING. I don't know why, but that doesn't seem to help.

DOCTOR. Love is a madness.

MARIE (*to the King*) Love *is* madness. And if you're mad with love, if you love blindly, completely, death will steal away. If you love me, if you love everything, love will consume your fear. The whole universe is one, everything lives again and the cup that was drained is full.

(*The* KING *looks under his blankets*)

KING. I'm full, all right, but full of holes. It makes me dizzy. I'm coming to an end.

MARIE. There is no end. Others will love in your place and gaze at the sky for *you*.

KING. I'm dying.

MARIE. The younger generation's expanding the universe.

KING. I'm dying.

MARIE. Conquering new constellations.

KING. I'm dying.

MARIE. Boldly battering at the gates of Heaven.

KING. They can knock them flat for all I care.

MARIE. You were a pioneer, a guide, a harbinger of all these new developments. You count. And you will be counted. You are inscribed for ever in the annals of the Universe.

KING. Who's going to look up the archives? I die, so let everything die. No, let everything stay as it is. No, if my death won't resound through worlds without end, let everything die. No, let everything remain.

GUARD. His Majesty the King wants the remains to remain.

KING. No, let it all die.

GUARD. His Majesty the King wants it all to die.

KING. Let it all die with me. No, let it all survive me. Let it all stay as it is. No, let it all die, stay, die, stay, die.

MARGUERITE. He doesn't know *what* he wants. (*She moves up* RC)

JULIETTE. I don't think he knows what he wants *any more*. (*She crosses to* L)

DOCTOR (*moving to* L *of Marguerite*) He no longer *knows* what he wants. His brain's degenerating, he's senile, gaga.

GUARD (*announcing*) His Majesty the King has gone ga . . .

MARGUERITE (*interrupting; to the Guard*) Idiot, be quiet. We want no more doctor's bulletins given to the press.

GUARD (*announcing*) Doctor's bulletins suspended by order of Her
Majesty Queen Marguerite.

(*The* KING *looks at* MARIE *who moves above the wheel-chair and puts
her arms around the King from behind*)

MARIE. My King, my little King.

KING. When I had nightmares and cried in my sleep, you would
wake me up, kiss me and smooth away my fears.

MARGUERITE. She can't do that, now.

KING. When I had sleepless nights and wandered out of my room
you would wake up, too, In your pink-flowered dressing-gown, you'd
come and find me in the throne room, take me by the hand and lead
me back to bed.

JULIETTE. It was just the same with *my* husband.

KING (*to Marie*) I used to share my colds with you, and the 'flu.

MARGUERITE. You won't catch colds, now.

KING (*to Marie*) We used to think the same things at the same
time. And you'd finish a sentence I'd just started in my head. And
you'd choose my ties for me. Though I didn't always like your
choice. We used to fight about that.

DOCTOR. A storm in a tea-cup.

MARGUERITE. How very suburban! We'll have to keep that out
of the Chronicles.

KING (*to Marie*) Then you'd dust my crown and polish the pearls
to make them shine.

MARIE (*moving to* L *of the King and kneeling beside him*) Do you love
me? Do you love me? I've always loved *you*. Do you still love me?
He *does* still love me. Do you love me today? Do you love me this
minute? Here I am. Here. I'm here. Look. Look. Please *look* at me.

KING. I've always loved myself, at least I can still love myself,
feel myself, see myself, contemplate myself.

DOCTOR (*looking at his watch*) He's running late—he's turned back
in his tracks.

MARGUERITE. It's not serious. Don't worry, Doctor, Executioner.
His little tricks, these kicks against the pricks— it was all to be
expected, all part of the programme.

DOCTOR. If this was a good old heart attack, we wouldn't have
had so much trouble.

MARGUERITE. Heart attacks are reserved for business men.

DOCTOR. Or even double pneumonia.

MARGUERITE. That's for the poor, not for Kings.

KING. I could decide not to die.

(MARGUERITE *moves to* R *of the King*)

JULIETTE. You see, he's not cured, yet.

KING. What if I decided to stop wanting things—(*he turns to
Marguerite*) and decided not to decide?

MARGUERITE. We would decide for you.

GUARD (*announcing*) The Queen and the Doctor will now make decisions for His Majesty the King.

DOCTOR. It is our duty.

(MARGUERITE *moves to her throne and sits. The* DOCTOR *moves to* R *of Marguerite.* MARIE *rises and moves down* L. JULIETTE *moves to the wheel-chair and pushes it, with the* KING *still in it, around the stage. The* GUARD *moves down* C)

GUARD. It was His Majesty, my Commander-in-Chief, who set the Thames on fire. It was he who invented gunpowder and stole fire from the gods. He nearly blew the whole place up. But he caught the pieces and tied them together again with string. I helped him, but it wasn't so easy. *He* wasn't so easy, either.

(JULIETTE *pushes the King* R)

He was the one who fitted up the first forges on earth. He discovered the way to make steel. He used to work eighteen hours a day. And he made *us* work even harder. He was our chief engineer.

(JULIETTE *pushes the King* L)

As an engineer, he made the first balloon, and then the Zeppelin. And finally, with his own hands, he built the first aeroplane. At the start, it wasn't a success. The first test pilots, Icarus and the rest, all fell into the sea. Till eventually he piloted the plane himself.

(JULIETTE *pushes the King* R)

I was his mechanic. Long before that, when he was only a little prince, he'd invented the wheelbarrow. I used to play with him. Then sails and railways and automobiles. He drew up the plans for the Eiffel Tower, not to mention his designs for the sickle and the plough——

(JULIETTE *pushes the King* L)

—the harvesters and the tractors.

KING. Tractors? Good Heavens, yes. I'd forgotten.

GUARD. He extinguished volcanoes and caused new ones to erupt. He built Rome, New York, Moscow and Geneva. He *founded* Paris. He created revolutions, counter-revolutions, religion, reform and counter-reform.

JULIETTE (*pushing the King* R) You wouldn't think so to look at him.

GUARD. He wrote the *Iliad* and the *Odyssey*.

KING. What's an automobile?

JULIETTE. It runs along by itself.

GUARD. He wrote tragedies and comedies, under the name of William Shakespeare.

JULIETTE. Oh, so that's who Shakespeare was.

DOCTOR. You ought to have told us ages ago.

GUARD. It was a secret. He invented the telephone and the telegraph, and fixed them up himself. He did everything with his own hands.

JULIETTE. He was never any good with his hands. (*She moves* RC) At the slightest sign of a leak he used to call the plumber.

GUARD (*moving to* L *of Juliette*) My Commander-in-Chief was a very handy man.

JULIETTE. Now he can't even get his shoes on. Or off.

GUARD. Not so long ago he managed to split the atom.

JULIETTE. Now he can't even turn the light off. Or on.

GUARD (*crossing above Juliette and the wheel-chair to* R *of the King*) Majesty, Commander-in-Chief, Master, Managing Director . . .

MARGUERITE (*to the Guard*) We know all about his earlier exploits. We don't need an inventory.

(*The* GUARD *returns to his post* R. JULIETTE *pushes the King up* LC)

KING (*while he is being pushed*) What's a horse? Those are windows, those are walls and this is the floor. I've done such things. What do they say I did? I don't remember what I did. I forget, I forget.

(JULIETTE *pushes the King up* C)

And that's a throne.

MARIE. Do you remember me? I'm here, I'm here.

(JULIETTE *pushes the King* C *and turns the wheel-chair to face front*)

KING. I'm here. I exist.

JULIETTE. He doesn't even remember what a horse is.

KING. I remember a little ginger cat.

MARIE. He remembers a cat.

(*The following lines about the cat should be spoken with as little emotion as possible: to say it, the* KING *should rather give the impression of being dazed, in a kind of dreamy stupor, except perhaps in the very last speech, which expresses a certain sorrow*)

KING. I used to have a little ginger cat. We called him our Wandering Jew. I found him in a field, stolen from his mother— (*he looks at Marguerite*) a real wild cat. He was two weeks old, but he knew how to scratch and bite. I fed him and petted him and took him home and he grew into the gentlest of cats. Once, madame, he crept into the coat-sleeve of a lady visitor. He was beautifully mannered, like a prince. When he got home in the middle of the night, he used to come and greet us with his eyes full of sleep. Then he'd stumble off back to his box. In the morning he'd wake us up to crawl into our bed. He was scared stiff of the vacuum cleaner. A bit of a coward, really, that cat; defenceless, a poet cat. I tried to introduce him to the outside world. I put him down on the pavement near the window. He was terrified, afraid of the pigeons that hopped all around him. There he was, pressed against the wall, miaowing and crying to me in desperation. To him, other animals and cats were strange creatures he mistrusted or enemies he feared. He only felt at home with us. We were his family. He thought we were cats and cats were something else. And yet one fine day he must have felt the urge to go out on his own. The neighbour's big dog killed him. And there he was, like a toy cat, a twitching marionette with one eye gone and a paw torn off, yes, like a doll destroyed by a sadistic child.

MARIE (*to Marguerite*) You shouldn't have left the door open; I warned you.

MARGUERITE. How I hated that sentimental, timorous beast.

KING. He was good and beautiful and wise, all the virtues. He loved me. My one and only cat.

DOCTOR. I repeat—he's running late.

MARGUERITE. I'm watching it. The time-table allows for hold-ups. Some delays were expected, you know.

KING. I used to dream about him—that he was lying in the grate, on the glowing embers, and Marie was surprised he didn't burn. I told her, "Cats can't burn, they're fireproof." He came miaowing out of the fireplace in a cloud of thick smoke. But it wasn't him any more. What a transformation! It was a different cat, fat and ugly. An enormous she-cat. Like his mother, the wild cat. A bit like Marguerite.

(JULIETTE *wheels the King down* C, *turns the wheel-chair to face up stage, then stands* L *of it.* MARGUERITE *rises and stands up* R *of the King.* MARIE *moves and stands down* L *of him. The* DOCTOR *moves and stands down* R *of Marguerite*)

JULIETTE. It's a great pity, I must say, a real shame. He was such a good King.

DOCTOR. Far from easy to please. Quite wicked, really. Revengeful and cruel.

MARGUERITE. Vain.

JULIETTE. There have been worse.

MARIE. He was gentle, he was tender.

GUARD. We were rather fond of him.

DOCTOR (*to the Guard and Juliette*) You both complained about him, though.

JULIETTE. That's forgotten, now.

DOCTOR (*moving above the King*) He was hard and severe and not even just.

GUARD (*moving to* R *of Marguerite*) He was strong. It's true he cut a few heads off.

JULIETTE. Not many.

GUARD. All for the public good.

DOCTOR. And the result? We're surrounded by enemies. And it's all his fault. He never cared what came after him. He never thought about his successors. After him, the deluge. Worse than the deluge, after him, there's nothing. Selfish bungler. (*He moves down* R)

JULIETTE. *"De mortuis nihil nisi bonum."* He was King of a great kingdom.
MARIE. He was the heart and centre of it.
JULIETTE. Its royal residence.
GUARD. A kingdom that stretched for thousands of miles around. You couldn't even glimpse its boundaries.
JULIETTE. Boundless in space.
MARGUERITE (*moving above the King*) But bounded in time. At once infinite and ephemeral.

(*The* GUARD *moves to* R *of Marguerite*)

JULIETTE. He was its Prince. its First Gentleman, he was its father and son. He was crowned King at the very moment of his birth.
MARIE. He and his kingdom grew up together.
MARGUERITE. And vanish together.
MARIE. The very day he was born, he created the sun.
JULIETTE. And that wasn't enough. He had to have fire made, too.
MARGUERITE. And there were wide open spaces, and there were stars, and the sky and the oceans and mountains; and there were plains, there were cities, and people and faces and buildings and rooms and beds; and the light and the night, and there were wars and there was peace.
GUARD. And a throne.
MARIE. And his fingers.
MARGUERITE. The way he looked and the way he breathed.
JULIETTE. He's still breathing, now.
MARIE. He's still breathing, because I'm here.
MARGUERITE (*to the Doctor*) Is he still breathing?
JULIETTE. Yes, Your Majesty. He's still breathing, because we're here.

(*The* GUARD *moves a little* R. *The* DOCTOR *bends over the King,* R *of him*)

DOCTOR. Yes, yes, no doubt about it. He's still breathing. His kidneys have stopped functioning, but the blood's still circulating. Going round and round. (*He moves above the King and uses his stethoscope*) His heart is sound.
MARGUERITE. It'll have to stop soon—what's the good of a heart that has no reason to beat?
DOCTOR. Exactly! His heart's gone berserk. D'you hear?

(*The frantic beatings of the* KING'S *heart can be heard*)

There it is, racing away, then it slows down, then it's off again, as fast as it can go.

(*The beating of the* KING'S *heart shakes the room. The crack in the wall widens and others appear. A stretch of wall could collapse or vanish from sight*)

JULIETTE. Good God! Everything's falling to pieces. (*She crouches on the floor*)

(*The* GUARD *moves up* R)

MARGUERITE. A mad heart, a madman's heart.

DOCTOR. A heart in a panic. It's infectious. Anyone can catch it.

MARGUERITE (*to Juliette*) It'll be quiet in a moment.

DOCTOR. We know every phase of the disease. It's always like this when a universe snuffs out.

MARGUERITE (*to Marie*) It proves his universe is not unique.

(*The heartbeats fade and stop. The* GUARD *moves down* R)

JULIETTE (*rising*) That never entered his head.

MARIE. He's forgetting me. At this very moment he's forgetting me. I can feel it, he's leaving me behind. I can't go on living if I don't exist in his distracted heart. (*She moves to* L *of the King*) Hold tight, hold firm! Clench your fists with all your strength. Don't let go of me. It's I who keep you alive. I keep *you* alive, you keep *me* alive. If you forget me, if you abandon me, I no longer exist, I am nothing.

DOCTOR. He will be a page in a book of ten thousand pages in one of a million libraries which has a million books.

JULIETTE. It won't be easy to find that page again. He's clenching his fists. He's hanging on. He's still resisting. He's coming back to consciousness.

MARIE (*to the King*) Hold me tight, as I hold you. Look at me, as I look at you.

(*The* KING *looks at Marie*)

MARGUERITE (*moving to* R *of the King*) She's getting you all mixed up. Forget about her and you'll feel better.

DOCTOR (*bending over the King*) Give in, Your Majesty. Abdicate, Majesty.

(JULIETTE *turns the wheel-chair for the* KING *to face* MARIE *who is* L *of it*)

KING. I can hear, I can see. Who are you? Are you my mother? My sister? My wife? My daughter? My niece? My cousin?

(JULIETTE *turns the wheel-chair for the* KING *to face* MARGUERITE *who is* R *of it*)

I know *you*. I'm sure I *do* know you. You hateful, hideous woman. Why are you still with me? Go away, go away!

MARIE. Don't look at her. Turn your eyes on me, and keep them wide open. Hope! I'm here. Remember who you are. I'm Marie.

(JULIETTE *turns the wheel-chair for the* KING *to face front*)

KING. Marie?

MARIE. If you don't remember, gaze at me and learn again that I am Marie. Look at my eyes, my face, my hair, my arms. And learn me off by heart.

MARGUERITE. You're upsetting him. He's past learning anything new, now.

MARIE (*to the King*) If I can't hold you back, at least turn and look at me. I'm here. Keep this picture of me in your mind and take it with you.

MARGUERITE. He could never drag that around, he hasn't got the strength. It's too heavy for a ghost. He's got to travel light. (*She bends over the King*) Throw everything away, lighten the load.

(*The* DOCTOR *draws the wheel-chair a little up* C)

DOCTOR. It's time he began to get rid of the ballast.

(*The* KING *pushes his blanket aside to* L)

Lighten the load, Your Majesty.

(*The* KING *rises, but he has a different way of moving, his gestures are jerky, he already begins to look rather like a sleep-walker. The movements of a sleep-walker will become more and more pronounced.* JULIETTE *takes the wheel-chair up* L. *The* DOCTOR *moves to* R *of the throne up* C)

KING. Marie?

MARGUERITE (*to Marie*) You see, your name means nothing to him, now.

GUARD. Marie's name now means nothing to the King.

KING. Marie! (*As he pronounces the name, he stretches out his arms and then lets them fall again*)

MARIE. He's said it.

DOCTOR. Repeated it, but without understanding.

JULIETTE. Like a parrot. Sounds that are dead.

KING (*moving to Marguerite*) I don't know you, I don't love you. (*He moves up* C)

(MARGUERITE *moves to* R *of the Doctor.* MARIE *sits on her throne*)

JULIETTE. He knows what not knowing means.

MARGUERITE (*to Marie*) He'll start his journey with a picture of *me* in his mind. That won't get in his way. It's fitted with a gadget that's worked by remote control. (*She moves* C. *To the King*) Have another look.

(*The* KING *looks out over the audience*)

MARIE. He can't see you.

MARGUERITE. He won't see *you* any more. (*She gestures towards Marie*)

(MARIE *suddenly disappears drawn off on her throne.* MARGUERITE *moves* RC)

JULIETTE (*moving down* L) He can't see any more.

(*The* DOCTOR *moves to* R *of the King and moves his finger back and forward in front of the King's eyes. The* KING *stares vacantly out over the audience*)

DOCTOR. That's true, he's lost his sight.

(*The* KING *moves slowly down* C, *advancing like a blind man, with very unsteady steps and his arms held out*)

GUARD. His Majesty is officially blind.

JULIETTE. He can hear. He's trying to listen, he's stretching out an arm, and now the other.

GUARD. What's he trying to take hold of?

JULIETTE. He wants something to lean on.

KING. Where are the walls? Where are the doors? Where are the windows?

JULIETTE (*moving to* L *of the King*) Here's an arm for you, Your Majesty.

(*The* KING *holds Juliette's arm*)

(*She leads the King to the wall* L) The walls are here, we are all here.

KING (*touching the wall*) The wall is here. (*He turns*) Guard, where are you? (*He crosses towards the Guard*) Answer me.

(JULIETTE *exits with the wheel-chair* LC *and re-enters moving on to the trap in the floor* L.)

GUARD. Still yours to command, Your Majesty. Yours to command.

(*The* KING *moves to the Guard and touches him*)

Yes, yes, I'm here. Yes, yes, I'm here.

JULIETTE. Your apartments are this way, Your Majesty.

(*The* KING *moves to* LC)

GUARD (*moving on to the trap in the floor* R) I swear we'll never leave your Majesty.

(*The* GUARD *suddenly disappears down the trap in the floor* R)

JULIETTE. We're here beside you, we'll stay with you.

(JULIETTE *disappears down the trap*)

KING. Guard! Juliette! Answer me! I can't hear you any more. Doctor, Doctor, am I going deaf?

DOCTOR. No, Your Majesty, not yet.

KING. Doctor!

DOCTOR. Forgive me, Your Majesty, I must go. I'm afraid I have to. I'm very sorry, please forgive me.

(*The* DOCTOR *backs out up* R, *bowing like a marionette, and still excusing himself*)

KING. His voice is getting faint and the sound of his footsteps is fading—he's gone.

MARGUERITE. He's a doctor, with professional obligations.

KING (*stretching out his arms*) Where are the others? (*He moves to the door down* R *and feels around it*) They've gone and they've shut me in.

MARGUERITE. They were a nuisance, all those people.

(*The* KING *moves* C. *He is walking rather more easily*)

They were in your way, hanging round you, getting under your feet. Admit they got on your nerves.

KING. I need their services.

MARGUERITE. I'll take their places. I'm the Queen of all Trades.

KING. I didn't give anyone permission to go. Make them come back.

MARGUERITE. They've been cut off. It's what you wanted.

KING. It's not what I wanted.

MARGUERITE. They could never have gone away if you hadn't wanted them to. You can't go back on your decision, now. You've dropped them!

KING (*turning to face up* C) Call them!

MARGUERITE. You've even forgotten their names. What were they called?

(*The* KING *is silent*)

How many were there?

KING (*turning*) Who do you mean? I don't like being shut in. Open the doors.

MARGUERITE (*moving to* R *of the King*) A little patience. The doors will soon be open wide.

(*There is a silence. The* KING *moves* LC)

KING. The doors—the doors—what doors?

MARGUERITE. Were there once some doors? Was there once a world, were you ever alive?

KING. I am. (*He moves* L)

MARGUERITE. Keep still. Moving tires you.

(*The* KING *is still*)

KING. I am. Sounds, echoes, coming from a great distance, fainter and fainter, dying away. I am deaf.

MARGUERITE (*moving to* R *of the King*) You can still hear *me*.

(*The* KING *stands silent and motionless*)

Sometimes you have a dream. And you get involved, you believe in it, you love it. In the morning, when you open your eyes, the two

worlds are still confused. The brilliance of the light blurs the faces of
the night. You'd like to remember, you'd like to hold them back.
But they slip between your fingers, the brutal reality of the day
drives them away. "What did I dream about?" you ask yourself.
"What was it happened? Who was I kissing? Who did I love? What
was I saying and what was I told?" Then you find you're left with a
vague regret for all those things that were or seemed to have been.
You no longer know what it was that was there all round you. You
no longer know.

KING. I no longer know what there was all round me. I know I
was part of a world, and this world was all about me. I know it was
me, but what else was there—what else?

MARGUERITE (*moving up* R) There are still some cords that bind
you which I haven't yet untied. Or which I haven't cut. There are
still some hands that cling to you and hold you back.

KING. Me. Me. Me.

MARGUERITE. This you is not the real you. (*She moves to* R *of the
King*) It's an odd collection of bits and pieces, horrid things that live
on you like parasites. The mistletoe that grows on the bough is not
the bough, the ivy that climbs the wall is not the wall. You're sagging
under the load, your shoulders are bent, that's what makes you feel
so old. And it's that ball and chain dragging at your feet which
makes it so difficult to walk. (*She bends and removes an imaginary ball
and chain from the King's feet, and as she straightens up she looks as though
she were making a great effort to lift the weight*) A ton weight, they must
weigh at least a ton. (*She pretends to throw the ball and chain in the direction of the audience, then, freed of the weight, she straightens up*) That's
better! How did you manage to trail them around all your life!

(*The* KING *tries to straighten up*)

And I used to wonder why you were so round-shouldered. It's
because of that sack. (*She pretends to take a sack from the King's shoulders
and throws it off* R) And that heavy pack. (*She pretends to take a pack from
the King's back and throws it off* R) And that spare pair of army boots.

KING. No!

MARGUERITE. Don't get so excited! (*She takes the imaginary boots
and throws them off* R) You won't need an extra pair of boots, any
more. Or that rifle, or that machine-gun. (*She takes the imaginary
weapons and puts them* R) Or that tool-box. (*She puts the imaginary tool-
box* R)

(*The* KING *protests*)

He seems quite attached to it. A nasty rusty old sabre. (*She removes
the imaginary sabre and puts it* R)

(*The* KING *tries grumpily to stop her*)

Leave it all to me and be a good boy. (*She taps on the King's hand*)
You don't need self-defence any more. No-one wants to hurt you,

now. (*She moves up* R *of the King*) All those thorns and splinters in your cloak, those creepers and seaweed and slimy wet leaves. How they stick to you. I'll pick them off, I'll pull them away. What dirty marks they made. (*She goes through the motions of picking and pulling them off*) The dreamer comes out of his dream. There you are! Now I've got rid of all those messy little things that worried you. Now your cloak's more beautiful, we've cleaned you up. You look much better for it. (*She extends her left hand to the King*) Now have a little walk. Give me your hand, give me your hand, then. Don't be afraid any more, let yourself go. I'll see you don't fall. You don't dare.

KING (*in a kind of stammer*) Me.

MARGUERITE. Oh, no. (*She crosses down* L) He imagines he's *everything*. He thinks *his* existence is *all* existence. I'll have to drive *that* out of his head. (*She crosses to* R *of the King. As if to encourage him*) Nothing will be forgotten. It's all safe in a mind that needs no memories. A grain of salt that dissolves in water doesn't disappear: it makes the water salty. (*She moves* R) Ah, that's it. Straighten up. Now you're not round-shouldered, no more pains in your back, no more stiffness. Wasn't it a heavy weight to bear? Now you feel better. You can go forward, now, go on. (*She moves to* R *of him*) Come along, give me your hand.

(*The* KING'S *shoulders slowly round again*)

Don't hunch your shoulders, you've no more loads to bear. Oh, those conditioned reflexes, so hard to shake off. You've no more weight on your shoulders, I tell you. (*She pats his back*) Stand up straight. Your hand . . .

(*The* KING *is undecided and clenches his right fist*)

How disobedient he is. Don't clench your fist like that. Open your fingers out. What are you holding? (*She takes the King's hand and opens it*) He's holding the whole kingdom in his hand. In miniature; on microfilm—in tiny grains. (*She releases his hand*)

(*The* KING *clenches his fist*)

That grain won't grow again, it's bad seed. Mouldy. Drop them. Unclasp your fingers. I order you to loosen those fingers. Let go of the plains, let go of the mountains. (*She opens the King's hand*) Like this. They were only dust. (*She tries to pull him* R) Come along. Still trying to resist. Where does he find all this will-power?

(*The* KING *bends forward*)

No, don't try to lie down.

(*The* KING *bends backwards*)

Don't sit down, either. No reason why you should stumble. I'll guide you, don't be frightened.

(*The* KING *takes her hand and starts to move down* R)

You can do it now, can't you? It's easy, isn't it? I've had a gentle slope made for you. It gets steeper later on, but that doesn't matter. You'll have your strength back by then.

(*The* KING *turns his head to look up* C)

Don't turn your head to see what you'll never see again; think hard, concentrate on your heart, keep right on, you must.

(*The* KING, *his eyes closed, turns and crosses to* L, *still held by the hand*)

KING. The Empire—has there ever been another empire like it? With two suns, two moons and two heavens to light it. And there's another sun rising, and there's another. A third firmament appearing, shooting up and fanning out. As one sun sets, others are rising—dawn and twilight all at once. Beyond the seven hundred and seventy-seven poles.

MARGUERITE (*leading him* C) Go farther, farther, farther. Toddle on, toddle on, go on.

KING. Blue, blue.

MARGUERITE (R *of the King*) He can still distinguish colours. Give up this Empire, too. And give your colours up. They're leading you astray, holding you up. You can't linger any longer, you can't stop again, you mustn't. (*She turns the King to face up stage and releases him*) Walk by yourself. (*She backs slowly to the throne up* C) Don't be frightened. Go on. It's the day, now, or the night, there's no more day and no more night. Try and follow that wheel that's spinning round in front of you. Don't lose sight of it, follow it. But not too close, it's all in flames, you might get burnt. Go forward. I'll move the undergrowth aside. Watch out! Don't bump into that phantom on your right—clutching hands, imploring hands, pitiful arms and hands, don't you come back, away with you! (*She moves up* R) Don't touch him, or I'll strike you. (*To the King*) Don't turn your head. Skirt the precipice on your left, and don't be afraid of that howling wolf—his fangs are made of cardboard, he doesn't exist. Wolf, cease to exist! Don't be afraid of the rats, now, either. They can't bite your toes. Rats and vipers, cease to exist! And don't start pitying that beggar, who's holding out his hand. Beware of that old woman coming towards you. Don't take that glass of water she's offering. You're not thirsty. He's no need to quench his thirst, old woman, he's not thirsty! Don't stand in his way! Vanish! Climb over the fence—that big truck won't run over you, it's a mirage—cross now. Why, no, daisies don't sing, even in the spring. I'll smother their cries. I'll obliterate them! And stop listening to the babbling of that brook. It's not real, anyway, it's deceiving you. False voices, be still! No-one's calling you, now. Smell that flower for the last time, then throw it away. Forget its perfume. Now you've lost the power of speech. Who's left for you to talk to?

(*The* KING *moves slowly towards the throne up* C)

Yes, that's right. Put your best foot forward. Now the other. There's a footbridge. No, you won't feel giddy. Hold yourself straight. You don't need your stick, besides, you haven't got one. Don't bend down and whatever you do, don't fall.

(*The* KING *starts to climb the steps of the throne*)

Up, up you go. Higher, up again, up you go, still higher, higher, higher.

(*The* KING *reaches the throne*)

(*She moves* C) Now, turn and face me.

(*The* KING *turns and faces Marguerite*)

Look at me. Look right through me. Gaze into my unreflecting mirror and stand up straight. (*She moves* R *and turns*) Give me your legs. The right one. Now the left.

(*As* MARGUERITE *gives him these orders, the* KING *stiffens his legs. The doors, windows and walls of the throne-room slowly disappear. This part of the action is very important*)

Give me a finger. Give me two fingers—three, four—five—all ten fingers. Now let me have your right arm. Your left arm. Your chest, your two shoulders and your stomach.

(*The* KING *is motionless, still as a statue*)

There you are, you see. (*She moves to the throne* RC) Now you've lost the power of speech, there's no need for your heart to beat, no more need to breathe. (*She sits on her throne*) It was a lot of fuss about nothing, wasn't it? Now you can take your place.

The KING *sits on his throne. The lights fade except for a greyish light around the King.*

MARGUERITE *is withdrawn on her throne* RC. *Now there is nothing on the stage except the* KING *on his throne. The throne revolves and the* KING *disappears. The disappearance of the windows, the doors and the walls, the* KING *and the thrones, must be very marked, but happen slowly and gradually. The* KING *sitting on his throne, should remain visible for a short time before finally, there is nothing but the grey light or mist and the empty throne with the crown and sceptre beneath.*

CURTAIN

FURNITURE AND PROPERTY PLOT

On stage: Revolving rostrum c. *On it:* throne with canopy

Throne (RC)

Throne (LC)

On floor: cigarette ends

Radiator (down R)

Radiator (down L)

Off stage: Halberd (GUARD)

Sceptre (KING)

Labels for thrones (GUARD)

Milk bucket, broom, duster (JULIETTE)

Telescope (DOCTOR)

King's slippers (JULIETTE)

Wheel-chair. *In it:* blanket, nightcap, hot-water bottle, bag for
sceptre and crown (JULIETTE)

White cap and apron (JULIETTE)

Personal: MARIE: handkerchief

JULIETTE: 2 clean handkerchiefs, Kleenex tissues, needle and
thread

DOCTOR: magnifying glass on cord, watch and chain, old-
fashioned stethescope

EFFECTS PLOT

Cue 1   GUARD: "His Majesty the King."   (Page 8)
Royal music

Cue 2   JULIETTE: "Shouting won't help."   (Page 21)
Distant echo "The King is going to die."

Cue 3   JULIETTE: "There's no-one there."   (Page 21)
Distant echo "Help!"

Cue 4   KING: "A fanfare!"   (Page 29)
Fanfare in the distance

Cue 5   DOCTOR: "D'you hear?"   (Page 39)
Sound of frantic heart-beats

Cue 6   MARGUERITE: ". . . is not unique."   (Page 40)
Heart-beats fade and stop

PRINTED IN GREAT BRITAIN BY
WHITSTABLE LITHO, STRAKER BROTHERS LTD.